Engaging with Spirituality in the Classroom

Applying Charlotte Mason's
Theological Anthropology
to Current Educational Practice
in a Secular Age

Elliott Shaw, PhD

Deani Van Pelt, PhD, series editor

CHARLOTTE
MASON
INSTITUTE

Series editor: Deani Van Pelt
Copy editors: Angie McCauley and Janelle Mills
Book/cover design and typesetting: Sharon Schnell, Terri Shown, Jody E. Skinner

This multi-authored monograph series, commissioned in connection with the Charlotte Mason Centenary, is designed to highlight and explore the continuing educational and leadership relevance of the late 19th-century British educationalist Charlotte Mason (1842–1923) through the collective contributions of the Armitt Museum and Library, the University of Cumbria, the Charlotte Mason Institute, and other scholars and practitioners worldwide.

Foreword

to the Charlotte Mason Centenary Series

Fewer than three decades ago a global surge of interest in the educational ideas of Charlotte Mason would have been unimaginable. Yet today, the design for education proposed by this late 19th and early 20th century educationalist is taking hold and influencing the teaching and learning of thousands of students and educators worldwide.

When we began discussing this series in early 2020, we sensed the potential of renewed scholarly focus on the writings and practices proposed by Charlotte Mason (1842-1923) but we did not anticipate how quickly the interest in her approach would be accelerated. The pandemic disruption of traditional classroom-based learning—and subsequent time spent exploring and experiencing alternatives—has resulted in many parents, teachers, students, school leaders, and policymakers, asking probing foundational questions—with unprecedented urgency and passion—about education.

With thousands of searches landing on the ideas of Charlotte Mason and so many schools, homeschools, and educational cooperatives now being started around her philosophy and practices, this multi-authored series release is aptly timed. In it, a diversity of researchers, scholars, and practitioners have come together around one question: *what is the enduring legacy and relevance of Charlotte Mason for education today?*

The Centenary Series is a collaboration among the Charlotte Mason Institute, the Armitt Museum and Library, and the University of Cumbria. It was birthed as a project of the university's Charlotte Mason Studies program which, through its appointments of Visiting Research Fellows, results in international collaborative research, writing, and conferencing, that connects Charlotte Mason's legacy with education today.

The monograph you hold in your hand is one of eighteen, written by a diverse group of education professors, researchers, classroom teachers, parents, and priests from Canada, the USA, and the UK. Their widely varied backgrounds, experience, and areas of expertise offer readers different lenses through which Mason might be viewed today. We believe that taking this broad approach is an important step in bringing Mason's ideas into the realm of mainstream discourse.

The series includes monographs that address Mason's biography and offer inviting overviews of her educational theory. Some offer a more philosophical, theological, historical, moral, or anthropological analysis, while others delve deeply into specific aspects of pedagogy such as narration, living books, outdoor education, assessment, or nature journaling. Each draws on the intersection of the author's field and an aspect of Mason's biography or philosophy and practice.

We hope that this series will stimulate further research and study of key relevant Mason principles and practices for learning, education, and development today. In one sense, the series optimizes and capitalizes on Ambleside as a critical place—an international hub—for the research and study of Mason. On the Ambleside campus of the University of Cumbria, one experiences the place where Mason lived and worked from 1894-1923. Within the Armitt Museum's collection, located at the base of the Ambleside campus, one finds the Charlotte Mason Collection featuring documents and artifacts from Mason and the institutions she founded. Indeed, each monograph includes at least one artifact from the Armitt Collection and, with sufficient notice, is available for public access. In another sense, this series recognizes that Mason's ideas have again taken hold across the world with international scholars and educators making her ideas their own and enriching the lives and experiences of children everywhere, most of whom will never step foot in Ambleside. Thus, while Ambleside is a natural destination for understanding and exploring Mason, it is hoped that this series will encourage more widespread study and engagement and continued conversation about the ideas of Mason's potentially vitalizing approach to relational education.

The Charlotte Mason Institute, with its long relationship with the Armitt and with the Ambleside Campus of the University of Cumbria, has generously contributed to this project through its role as publisher. CMI saw the promise in convening a wide variety of experts and has been an encouragement throughout. Our deepest gratitude goes to Prof. Lois Mansfield, Campus Director of the Ambleside Campus of the University of Cumbria, without whose tenacious vision, neither this project nor the other appointments and events that accompany its release would have happened. Faye Morrisey, Manager and Curator at The Armitt Museum and Library, was a tireless supporter of this project, ever ready to encourage the authors and editors and provide ready access to documents and artifacts when needed. Jody Skinner, Terri Shown, Sharon Schnell, Angie McCauley and Janelle Mills have generously provided endless support with layout, cover design, and copy editing. This project would not have come to be without their continuous persistent dedication. Kristen Forney's administrative support was invaluable as a project of this scale contains so many moving components. Our peer reviewers and project advisors were integral to this series and we are grateful for the privilege of working with so many kind and insightful colleagues in the field. My sincerest thanks to Hilary Cooper and Sally Elton-Chalcraft for encouraging this series and for their support throughout.

And finally, none of this would have been possible without our authors and all those who supported each one giving them time and space to research and write. These authors were a joy to work with and their contributions add significantly to the research and analysis offered on the relevance of Charlotte Mason's design for education today. We look forward to the questions, insights, and renewal of education practice, that their words will provoke.

Deani Van Pelt, PhD
Series Editor
June 2023
Ottawa, Canada

Abstract

This piece seeks to examine the way in which Charlotte Mason understood the identity of the child, with particular reference to the child's perceived distinctive spiritual attributes. In keeping with a number of writers of the period, Mason viewed the child to have a particularly close connection to the divine and, thus, a privileged spiritual identity. For Mason, nature-based education was an important way to preserve the child's spirituality—first, because such education fosters a connection with nature and, second, because nature has a quasi-sacramental quality through its manifestation of divine creativity. This account of Mason's view of the spirituality of the child is contextualized within an examination of the broader cultural trends of the 19th century—such as the development of Liberal Protestantism, Darwinian evolution and Social Darwinism—and presents Mason's nature spirituality as in part a response to the challenges to faith posed by these cultural tendencies. Further to this my research seeks to situate Mason's view of the child within a broader historical trajectory of educational reflection on the spirituality of the child. Here it is proposed that the privileging of the child's spirituality, and the practice of presenting spirituality in contradistinction to prevailing cultural forces, aligns Mason's ideas to recent and contemporary views on childhood spirituality. While much useful work has been done on integrating spiritual awareness into teaching, there is arguably scope for a deeper understanding of the way in which theories about the place of childhood spirituality in education have developed over time. By situating Mason's thought within this context, it is hoped that this piece can facilitate a deeper understanding of this area for both practitioners and nonpractitioners, and provide a framework useful to teachers interested in teaching about spirituality in the classroom.

Contents

List of Figures

Introduction

If there were one book that could be considered to capture the religious *zeitgeist* of England in the late 19th century it would be Mrs. Humphrey Ward's best-selling novel *Robert Elsmere*. Inspired by the religious upheavals of the Victorian period, the novel recounts the course of the crisis of faith of the Anglican clergyman Robert Elsmere under the impact of the heterodox views of his college mentor, the Hegelian-minded Henry Grey, and his parish's "resident scholar, the arch-skeptic, Roger Wendover" (Cook, 2011, p. 108). Exposed through his associates to the radical biblical criticism of German Liberal Protestantism (Ward, 1888/1987), Elsmere loses his faith in the traditions of the church, resigns his pastorate, and devotes himself to social work among the poor and low educated in the slums of London. The novel ends tragically with Elsmere contracting tuberculosis and dying in Cairo.

Charlotte Maria Shaw Mason was among the many thousands who read, and felt the impact of, Ward's novel. Her personal response took the form of an unpublished fictional letter, written under the pseudonym May Hendry, through which she conveyed her sense of dismay at Elsmere's transition from simple faith to the adoption of theological rationalism:

You know what a lovely Christ like life the young clergyman leads and how heavenly minded – even if a little
narrow – is the woman he marries. The first volume is
delightful – a story of kingdom come; pure earthly love,
ever waiting at the head waters of love, for inspiration
direction and loves of service: Though you already feel
there is a leak somewhere, and the enemy may any day
come in as a flood. Then, all at once with little to lead up
to it comes the catastrophe, a spiritual one. Elsmere is
bowled over, with hardly a struggle to keep his feet by so
stale an argument as that "miracles do not happen!" Then
follows a kind of land-slip bearing down all the bulwarks
of Christianity. Miracles do not happen; therefore the
Resurrection has not happened, therefore the Christians'
king is discrowned; God has not spoken to man and there
is no revelation. What is left? A forlorn hope that there
is a God, that if He be, He may be precious. (Mason,
1888/9, p. 5)

While Mason lamented Elsmere's loss of faith, her writings
might suggest that her faith position and the views of the later
Elsmere were not entirely antithetical. The movement to which
Elsmere devoted himself in his final years, the New Brotherhood
of Christ, was not based on biblical teaching or the doctrines of
Anglicanism but on a more perennial perspective of the divine
expressed through the "continuous and only revelation of God in
life and nature" (Ward, 1987, p. 555, as cited in Schork, 1989, p.
295). While Mason remained a devout adherent to Anglicanism
and a conscientious student of the Bible throughout her life, she

was an eclectic reader[1] whose theology reflected a disposition to embrace new knowledge and, from this perspective, to consider the presence of the divine to be mediated through nature and knowledge itself. Such an approach to faith was evident in her view that all truth originates from the Holy Spirit, "the supreme Educator of mankind" (Mason, 1886–1925/2008, p. 276), leading her to present knowledge acquisition as a form of spiritual practice. As Mason (1886–1925/2008) put it in her twenty principles of education:

> We allow no separation to grow up between the intellectual and 'spiritual' life of children, but teach them that the divine Spirit has constant access to their spirits, and is their continual helper in all the interests, duties and joys of life. (p. 9)

As was the case in Mason's time, there are many challenges in our day to the pursuit of a personal faith. In contrast to the challenges posed by the higher critical theories that called into question the historicity of the Bible, believers of today have to contend with a general decline in religious practice complemented by a militant new form of atheism which presents religious belief as irrational, harmful, and undermining of progressive,

---

1.   These are some of the figures whose ideas informed Mason's thought: educational theorists such as Jean-Jacques Rousseau, Johann Heinrich Pestalozzi, and Friedrich Froebel; scientists such as Thomas Huxley, Charles Darwin, and Herbert Spencer; cultural critics such as Thomas Carlyle, John Stuart Mill, and John Ruskin; theological writers such as F. D. Maurice, John Keble, and Eugène Bersier; and the poets Samuel Taylor Coleridge and William Wordsworth.

liberal values.[2] Mason's spiritual response to the challenges of 19th century liberalism was itself informed by a particular expression of theological anthropology.[3] Mason saw the child as one who had a privileged ability to appreciate the presence of the divine through the abundant beauty of nature. Accordingly, for Mason, a key role of education was to complement fact-based understanding of the natural environment with a sense of spiritual connection to nature. Such a goal is as relevant today as it was in Mason's time. Against the background of the environmental crisis and the challenges posed to faith traditions by movements such as new atheism, Mason's theological anthropology can inform a view of education based in a particular form of spiritual apprehension that aligns her work with that of present-day thinkers. An examination of the interconnection between Mason's theological anthropology and nature-based, spiritually-focused education can usefully be made with particular reference to Mason's Home Schooling Series and her *Scale How Meditations*, as well as her unpublished essay "The Ruling Conscience in the House of Body" and unpublished poem "Unto Us a Child is Born."

---

2. Key publications in the area of new atheism are: Sam Harris's *The End of Faith: Religion, Terror, and the Future of Reason* (2004), Daniel Dennett's *Breaking the Spell: Religion as a Natural Phenomenon* (2006), Richard Dawkins's *The God Delusion* (2006), Christopher Hitchens's *God Is Not Great: How Religion Poisons Everything* (2007), and A. C. Grayling's *The Good Book: A Secular Bible* (2011).
3. Theological anthropology is concerned with what it means to be human and the place of humans in understanding religious faith.

The Enlightenment and its Heritage

The later decades of the 18th century and the early decades of the 19th century were dominated by two great cultural movements: the Enlightenment and Romanticism. Whereas the former employed reason to challenge the authority of monarchies and established churches, the latter challenged the pure reason of the Enlightenment by promoting the empowering effects of feeling and imagination as the basis of liberation and life enhancement. Out of these movements a new theology emerged in the form of Liberal Protestantism. Reflecting the Enlightenment's commitment to individual freedom, Liberal Protestantism claimed that it was possible to have a personal faith without reference to external authority, be it the church, Scripture, or tradition.

Such a view was particularly evident in the work of David Friedrich Strauss (1808–1874). The publication in 1835 of Strauss's two-volume *Das Leben Jesu, kritisch bearbeitet*, rendered into English by George Eliot as *The Life of Jesus, Critically Examined* (1846), brought about a new dawn in biblical criticism. Sweeping aside even the rationalistic attempts of Kant and Hegel to preserve orthodoxy, Strauss argued that the supernaturalistic elements in the New Testament were expressions of a mindset informed by a mythological worldview (Harvey, 1961). In Strauss's mind, the myths of the New Testament were created and projected onto Jesus in order to connect Old Testament prophecy to the person of Jesus. In place of the virgin birth, miraculous events, the resurrection, and the ascension to heaven, Strauss offered a theology of divine immanence within humankind. Instead of the incarnate God whose death atoned for the sins of the world, Jesus became a purely human figure whose identity had been reshaped by the early Christian community (Linstrum, 2010).

Thirteen years after the publication of *The Life of Jesus*, orthodox theology was confronted with an additional challenge in the form of Charles Darwin's *On the Origin of Species* (1859). The theory at the heart of Darwin's work, that life evolved and adapted to its environment through natural selection, posed a number of fundamental challenges to Christian belief—for example, the place of Adam and Eve in the evolutionary process, how the doctrines of the fall and redemption were to be understood in an evolutionary context, and the nature of humanity as a special divinely ordained creation (Jones, 2012). For some, such as the biologist Thomas Henry Huxley and the physicist John Tyndall, the answer to such questions was that there was no scope for reconciliation. Supernaturalism had no place in science, and any attempt to reconcile evolution with orthodox Christianity was fallacious (Jones, 2012). Some in the church agreed with this principle of incompatibility, albeit for very different reasons. Thus, Samuel Wilberforce (1860), the Bishop of Oxford, denounced natural selection as "absolutely incompatible not only with single expressions in the word of God ... but ... with the whole representation of that moral and spiritual condition of man which is its proper subject matter" (pp. 257–258). For Wilberforce, the living world did not come about through natural selection but "is the transcript in matter of ideas eternally existing in the mind of the Most High" (p. 259). In a similar vein, the American Reformed Presbyterian theologian and Principal of Princeton Theological Seminary, Charles Hodge (1874), viewed Darwinian evolution as entailing the denial of design in nature and, therefore, as equivalent to the denial of divine providence.

Others, however, disagreed. The English Catholic biologist George Jackson Mivart (1871) argued that evolution was the instrument used by God to bring into being the multiplicitous forms which preexisted in the mind of God and that the human soul was a special nonmaterial creation. These ideas were met with approval by Bishop John Cuthbert Hedley (1871), who stated: "It has been too hastily assumed that the 'evolution' theory is a smashing assault upon orthodoxy that is carrying terror and confusion into the ranks of all believers in Revelation. It is nothing of the kind" (p. 3). Two years later the Scottish biologist and Free Church evangelist Henry Drummond published *Natural Law in the Spiritual World* (1873), in which he argued for the continuity of natural laws between the domains of matter and spirit. Here Drummond argued that evolution represented both a material and a spiritual process, which would culminate in the final unity of all things (Lightman, 2010). Finally, Geremia Bonomelli, Bishop of Cremona, saw in evolution the basis on which all living beings are united, describing it as a "stupendous, universal law which relates all the creatures one to another ... which creates order and beauty" (Bonomelli, as cited in Ayala, 2007, p. 227).

Mason's writings on the education of the child reveal her to have been acutely aware of the prevailing cultural debates of the period and wary of, even antipathetic towards, the Enlightenment project and its heritage. As she put it rather forcefully in the essay "The Ruling Conscience in the House of Body": "In our own days of Enlightenment progress we seem to be less aware of the grossness, dumbness, and foulness of ignorance than the thoughtful minds of the Middle Ages." Such apprehension was evident when she wrote in the same essay of history's "abundant evidence of the fallibility of reason" (Mason, n.d.-a). The criticism was given more precise form as Mason focused on the impact of John Locke's thought on European politics. Mason (1886–1925/2008) attributed what she identified as the "doctrine of the infallible reason"[4] (p. 247) to the undermining of traditional authority and the political turmoil across the channel:

> Locke was eagerly read because his opinions jumped with the thought of the hour. His principles were put into practice, his conclusions worked out to the bitter end, and thoughtful writers consider that this religious and cultivated English gentleman cannot be exonerated from a share of the guilt of the atrocities of the French Revolution (p. 247).

Mason's views on the harmful effects of secular philosophy were also addressed to Herbert Spencer, best known for coining the term "survival of the fittest" based on the application of Darwin's theory of natural selection to human society.[5] Mason

---

4. It should be noted that Locke did not use the phrase "doctrine of the infallible reason" in his writings. However, Locke did believe in the power of reason to enable the individual to grasp truth and to determine the effective functioning of government, as well as calling for the separation of church and state (one of the fundamental tenets of the French Revolution). See Locke's *Essay on Human Understanding* (1689) and *A Letter Concerning Toleration* (1689).
5. "This survival of the fittest, which I have here sought to express in mechanical terms, is that which Mr. Darwin has called 'natural selection', or the preservation of favored races in the struggle for life." (Spencer, 1864, pp. 444–445)

(1886–1925/2008) did not refer directly to this key concept but presented Spencer as one who recognized "that the enthronement of the human reason is the dethronement of the Almighty God" (pp. 247–248). This observation is possibly an oblique reference to Spencer's *First Principles* (1862), in which Spencer promulgated one of the earliest accounts of agnosticism, claiming that the limits of human knowledge mean that we cannot have any valid conception or knowledge of God. Mason (1886–1925/2008) concluded that this dethronement of God, reflected in Spencer's thought, would lead to the dethronement of human authority "whether it be of kings and their deputies over nations, or of parents over families" (p. 248).

Mason's concern over the socio-political overtones of Spencer's thought resonates with her general views on the direction of education in her time and the particular influence Spencer was exercising. Mason (1886–1925/2008) had a rather dim view of the state of education in her day, describing it as looking "rather bleak at home and abroad" (p. 138). The basis of this assessment was twofold. First, in Mason's (n.d.-a) eyes, education had become characterized by the inchoate acceptance of widely ranging ideas: "The ignorance at home, in our very schools and colleges, is a cause of alarm.... The very 'tolerance' upon which we pride ourselves arises from the ignorance which does not know how to distinguish between things that differ." Second, experts had sought to make schooling "more technical and utilitarian" without any "unifying principle," "definite aim" or "philosophy of education" (Mason, 1886–1925/2008, p. 138). It is here that Spencer's theory of the survival of the fittest and Mason's critique of education can be seen as possibly interconnecting. Spencer's perception of the human condition as characterized by the struggle for survival meant that, in Spencer's mind, education should be directed towards supporting those who were supposedly most worthy of survival. With this in mind, Spencer privileged the teaching of science over purportedly less practical disciplines, such as Latin and Greek, in order to facilitate the production of citizens capable of contributing to a world defined by industrial competition. (See Spencer's *Education: Intellectual, Moral and Physical* (1861).) To achieve his social agenda, Spencer advocated the very type of technical education which Mason so roundly denounced. For Mason, such an approach to teaching was not only undermining of education but socially harmful; the real danger of a technically based educational regime lay in its advocacy of unregulated competition over rule-based authority in the name of liberty. As Mason (1886–1925/2008) warned Spencer's would-be followers:

> They accept the philosopher's teaching when he bids them bring up children without authority in order to give them free room for self-development; without perceiving, or perhaps knowing, that it is the labour of the author's life to eliminate the idea of authority from the universe, that he repudiates the authority of parents because it is a link in the chain which binds the universe to God. (p. 248)

In the face of such an approach to education, Mason (1886–1925/2008) prescribed the restoration of authority, focusing on the divine as foundational to all authority and all authority-based systems (pp. 248–249).

Such wariness of the Enlightenment project, and its

philosophical heritage, is further evident in Mason's views on Liberal Protestantism, in particular concerning Liberal Protestantism's denial of the miraculous. Mason was clear that any attempt to deny miracles is positively harmful to faith and should be rejected. Describing the "whole superstructure of 'liberal' religious thought" as "miserably shaky," Mason (1886–1925/2008) treated any attempt to replace belief in the miraculous with a theology based in ethical teaching as undermining the cornerstone of faith: "Remove the keystone of miracle and the arch tumbles about our ears" (p. 170). In Mason's (1886–1925/2008) mind, the denial of miracles was tantamount to the denial of God's providential action and personal dealing with creation, and distanced the believer from God; miracles are important because they convey the attributes of God—such as grace and mercy—and underpin the nature of God's action in the world (p. 171). The challenge for Christians is to affirm belief in miracles in the face of skepticism. As Mason (1898/2011) put it in her *Scale How Meditations*, the Liberal Protestant denial of the historicity of miracles has changed the place of miracle within Christian narrative: where once belief in the miraculous provided support for faith it now constitutes a test of faith (p. 83).

Interestingly, while Mason unequivocally rejected the tenets of Liberal Protestantism, she was prepared at the same time to provisionally accept Darwinism. Mason (1886–1925/2008) was very much aware of the revolutionary change brought about by Darwin's theory of natural selection, describing such change as "the great bouleversement of thought" (p. 222) that "has made a great impression on the minds of men" (p. 223). In keeping with the views of figures such as Bonomelli, Mason

(1886–1925/2008) saw in evolution a process within which all life is interconnected (p. 223) and talked of "the enormous repose and satisfaction to the human mind contained in the idea of evolution" (p. 297).

This acceptance of the reconciliation of faith and science was, however, modified by two caveats. First, Mason was wary of the potential within Darwinism to support a materialist understanding of the mind and the implication of such an understanding for human identity:

> For five thousand years, at least, philosophers have been in search of a single principle which shall cover, to put it crudely, matter to mind. We think, today, that we have found this principle in evolution. It may be so, but we come to the conclusion without due knowledge of what has already been thought, without even taking in the fact that if we accept the doctrine of the evolution of mind, we give up the idea there is any life here or hereafter excepting physical life, any existence beyond a physical existence. (Mason, n.d.-a)

Second, Mason was unconvinced by the practice of systematically synthesizing evolution and Christianity. That this was the case is evident in a particular reference Mason (1898/2011) made to the work of Henry Drummond at the beginning of *The Scale How Meditations*: "some as in Natural Law in the Spiritual World try to make science and religion accord; and confess in the end that they have failed" (p. 38). In place of such attempted systematic integration, Mason (1898/2011) was willing to accept that there is a tension between the scientific and biblical narratives about the origins of life, in much the same way that there has been a historical tension in attempts to integrate belief and philosophy within Christian thought (p. 38).

This tension between science and faith informed Mason's views on how creation should be taught to children. Here Mason (1886–1925/2008) recommended children be introduced to the Genesis narrative of the creation and fall without commentary while allowing for the possibility of subsequent discussion of current scientific discoveries and archaeology (p. 92). In this spirit Mason advocated that Christian parents should not be fearful of allowing their children to be exposed to current scientific thought; in fact, according to Mason (1886–1925/2008), denying children access to scientific knowledge could in the longer term create distrust on the part of children towards Christian education (p. 297). Human advances in our understanding of the natural world should be treated as a form of "progressive revelation made by God" (Mason, 1886–1925/2008, p. 297); such a perspective on knowledge will foster both a reverential attitude to science and God and a mind open to new knowledge. With this in mind, Mason commended Canon Paterson Smyth's *Bible for the Young.*[6] In Mason's eyes, Patterson Smyth's commentary could be used to introduce children to modern criticism and the theory of evolution without undermining their belief in God as Creator.

---

6. John Patterson Smyth was an Anglican clergyman who produced a series of commentaries on the books of the Bible titled *The Bible for Home and School.*

Spirituality and Education:
Then and Now

So far, it has been established that, in engaging with the defining cultural forces of her time, Mason sought a balance between challenging modes of thinking that disturb faith while at the same time being open to new forms of scientific knowledge. Mason's wariness of the Enlightenment heritage, and its impact on education, raises the broader questions of how she viewed the nature of knowledge and the most appropriate way to impart knowledge to the child. For Mason (1886–1925/2008), knowledge had a profoundly spiritual dimension, for it is the Holy Spirit who is "the Imparter of knowledge, the instructor of youth, the inspirer of genius" (p. 227); as such it is the Holy Spirit who is at work in the education of the child in all academic disciplines. This view of the spirituality of knowledge is particularly evident in Mason's (1886–1925/2008) endorsement of what she identifies as the medieval position that all cultural progress can be attributed to the work of the Holy Spirit:

> But the Florentine mind of the Middle Ages went further than this: it believed, not only that the seven Liberal Arts were fully under the direct outpouring of the Holy Ghost, but that every fruitful idea, every original conception, whether in Euclid, or grammar, or music, was a direct inspiration from the Holy Spirit, without any thought at all as to whether the person so inspired named himself by the name of God, or recognised whence his inspiration came (p. 227).

The perception of knowledge as spiritual resonates with Mason's account of the special spiritual identity of small children, including the Christ child. The focus of Mason's (n.d.-b) poem "Unto Us a Child is Born" illustrates the power of the Christ child through a narrative that progresses from Mary lovingly and tenderly protecting the child to a conclusion which affirms Christ's omnipotent rule:

> All his rest is on her arm;
> She, his only shield from harm;
> She doth his sole meat supply;
> All his joy is in her eye.
>
> ....
>
> Other fearsome inmates there,
> Evil dragons, giant care;
> Hope, joyous, sees them led in thrall,
> This "Little One" shall rule them all!

The omnipotence of the Christ child reflects the privileged spiritual status of the small child who is deeply connected to the divine. Referring to Wordsworth's poem "Intimations of Immortality," Mason (1886–1925/2008) ascribed to the newborn child the residual presence of a "heavenly aroma," and connected the "heavenly atmosphere" surrounding the child's soul to Christ's teaching in Matthew's Gospel that we need to become like a child to enter heaven (p. 13). The spiritually privileged status of children is apparent in their innocence; the small child exists in a condition of unrealized moral potential, as can be noted from the second of Mason's (1886–1925/2008) home schooling principles: "They [children] are not born either good or bad, but with the possibilities for either good or evil" (p. 139). The enactment of these possibilities is governed by the exercise of the child's innate sense of right and wrong, mediated through the conscience: "Conscience is the spiritual sense that gives us knowledge of good and evil. A six-month old baby who isn't even speaking yet will show evidence of a conscience" (Mason, 1886–1925/2008, p. 120).

As the child grows, the role of education is both to guide in knowledge and good judgment and to enable the child to retain his or her deep elemental sense of spiritual connection (Mason, 1886–1925/2008). Here it is possible to identify the connection between teaching children about nature and cultivating the child's spiritual awareness. In the same way that one might esteem the author of a great book or the artist who has produced a great painting, so nature should be a source of reverence towards the divine:

> What daily and hourly thanks and praise, then, do we owe to the Maker and designer of the beauty, glory, and fitness above our heads and about our feet and surrounding us on every side! From the flower in the crannied wall to the glorious firmament on high, all the things of Nature proclaim without ceasing. (Mason, 1905/1921, p. 100)

The prescription that nature should foster reverence of the divine also informed Mason's exegesis of scriptural passages that use nature imagery. Christ's use of such imagery in his teaching is interpreted by Mason (1898/2011) to indicate that nature itself points to and reveals the divine: "every leaf on every tree is inscribed with the Divine name ... all nature is symbolic, or as has been better said, is sacramental" (p. 61). Nature provides a ubiquitous testimony to the divine presence: "God nowhere leaves himself without a witness ... every beauteous form and sweet sound is charged with teaching for us" (Mason, 1898/2011, p. 61). It is the failure on the part of some believers to connect with nature that led Mason (1886–1925/2008) to chide them for their lack of observance:

> He opens his mouth and draws in his breath for the delight he has in the law .... Towards the other laws of God which govern the universe he sometimes takes up an attitude of antagonism, almost of resistance, worthy of an infidel. (p. 23)

In order to preempt this state of affairs it is important that children should be educated to connect with and appreciate the world of nature through careful observation of small animal life and through the use of a nature notebook to record observations, all of which will support a lifelong appreciation of nature (Mason, 1886–1925/2008, pp. 28–9). This practice of recording nature can be seen in the following images from Margaret Deck's 1910–1911 nature notebook in the Charlotte Mason Collection at the Armitt Museum and Library:

FIGURE 1
Common Avens (1910)

FIGURE 2
Figwort (1910)

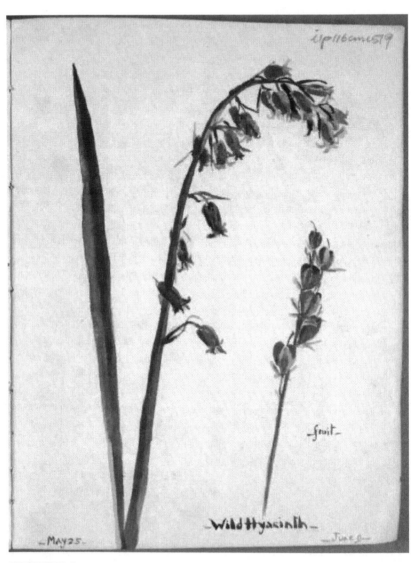

FIGURE 3
Wild Hyacinth (1911)

Mason's formation of a pedagogy that connects the spiritual development of the child to the observation of nature complements previous and later thinking about these areas of educational practice. Like Mason, Friedrich Froebel, the founder of the kindergarten movement, recognized the interconnection between exposure to nature and the child's spiritual well-being; Froebel sought to enact this vision through the provision of a garden-based educational setting for children in the hope that the child's attachment to nature would allow for the flourishing of "the divine essence within the child" (Wilson, 2010, p. 25). In a similar spirit, Mason's contemporary Maria Montessori viewed the child's immersion in the natural world as necessary for the healthy development of his or her essential nature (Bertolino & Filippa, 2021). Montessori's emphasis on sensory education (skill development through exploration of the senses) was reflected in her advocacy of the practice of enabling children to be exposed to the elements of nature through working in flower gardens or vegetable patches. Such an end, however, could only be achieved by aligning the sensibilities of the educator to that of the child. To enhance the development of the child's aesthetic imagination through such exposure, both the scientist and the teacher should share the child's fascination with nature and focus their "inquiry on the spirit of nature, and not just on its mechanisms" (Bertolino & Filippa, 2021). Further to this, the child's sense of connection with nature should inform an all-embracing sense of connection with the cosmos. As Aline Wolf put it:

> Essentially Montessori's cosmic education gives the child
> first an all-encompassing sense of the universe with its

billions of galaxies. Then it focuses on our galaxy, the Milky Way, our solar system, planet Earth and its geological history, the first specimens of life, all species of plants and animals and finally human beings. Inherent in the whole study is the interconnectedness of all creation, the oneness of things. (Wolf, 2004, as cited in Miller, 2010, p. 271)

More recently, a number of scholars have engaged with children's spirituality in response to the presence of cultural forces that are perceived to have impeded the spiritual self-expression of the child. David Hay and Rebecca Nye (2006) acknowledge the massive presence of spirituality in the lives of children while lamenting the condition of "culturally constructed forgetfulness" which has led to spirituality being "sidelined in the educational system" (p. 9).

In a similar vein, Tobin Hart (2003, 2004a) has affirmed the special spiritual insights of children that, in Hart's thinking, lie outside of adult cognition. For Hart (2003) the adult world's failure to acknowledge the spirituality of children is expressive of a long history of the suppression of the spiritual in favor of rational, linear thinking, beginning with the medieval dominance of Aristotelianism in logic, science, and theology, and "consolidated in the reformation or scientific revolution" (2004b, p. 29). In the modern period this tendency has been exacerbated by the Cartesian shift towards seeking certainty over wisdom (Hart, 2009), by the Freudian restrictive account of the mind which "underestimates the human" (Hart, 2009, p. 128), and by contemporary psychiatry's treatment of moments of inner guidance "as mere fantasy or, worse, as a sign not of divinity, but of pathology" (Hart, 2003, p. 215).

Like Hay and Nye, Hart (2004b) laments the sidelining of the spiritual in education. Reflecting society's marginalization of contemplative spirituality, education in the West has excluded the contemplative in favor of the rational, the empirical, the analytical, and the calculative. As a consequence of such exclusion our educational systems have failed to recognize how contemplation complements the rational and sensory approach to education (Hart, 2004b, 2009). This in turn has resulted in educators neglecting to use contemplation to enhance perceptual skills (Hart, 2004b) and the failure of educators to understand how contemplation can foster a sense of emotional intimacy with the object of study and, in turn, drive the motivation to learn (Hart, 2004b). Such failures have brought into being an educational regime which focuses primarily on the provision of information for the passing of tests, and which encourages children to be extrinsically motivated to learn to the detriment of their broader skill development (Hart, 2009); such a tendency is exacerbated by the existence in schools of a socially Darwinian culture of competition "in which only the fittest socially, emotionally, and intellectually survive" (Hart, 2009, p. 103). Where attempts to engage with children's spirituality have occurred, they have merely taken the form of encouraging children to think about the nature of God, based around adult-constructed categories of thought. As an antidote to this situation, we need to move beyond conceiving of children's spirituality through the medium of language about God (Hart, 2003) to a point where education begins from the perspective of the child (Hart, 2004a) and takes seriously the development of the child's inner life and spiritual capacity (Hart, 2003). Such practice would require teachers to be equipped to teach contemplation, find time and place for worship, and employ contemplative practice in the classroom (Hart, 2009).

Finally, like Hart, Marian de Souza (2016a) affirms the way in which spirituality complements the affective and the cognitive and laments the way in which education has neglected the spiritual. For de Souza (2016b) the recognition of the child as "an individual with a rational mind that thinks, an emotional mind that feels and a spiritual mind that intuits, imagines, wonders and creates," and worships is essential to fostering the full potential, capabilities and well-being of the child (p. 123). Such an account of spirituality is informed by a more developed recognition of the distinction between traditional faith-based spirituality (which is clearly connected to religious traditions and the quest for God) and non-God related spirituality in which there is a profound sense of connection with, for example, beauty or the creative process (de Souza, 2017). In this latter version of spirituality seekers are looking for "more holistic ways and means to engage and practise their spirituality so as to encompass the wholeness of their humanity" (de Souza, 2017, p. 3). This process requires "new ways and language to discuss, study, and understand human spirituality as something holistic and essential to the flourishing of human beings" (de Souza, 2017, p. 3). While these two versions of spirituality are grounded in very different worldviews, they are interconnected through the central place that relationality has within them. Those engaged in the spiritual quest are on a "relational continuum" (de Souza, 2018); the more one progresses along this continuum, the deeper is one's sense of connectedness, empathy, and compassion (de Souza, 2018).

Mason's engagement with children's spirituality, education, and nature can be seen as part of a continuum of thought which complements the work of other practitioners. While Mason was working within a specifically Christian framework, her thought anticipated the ideas of more recent advocates of religiously eclectic and secular-based approaches. Thus, Montessori's view that nature connects the child to the cosmos echoes Mason's view of nature as sacramentally mediating the divine. Mason's perception of a heavenly aroma around the small child resonates with de Souza's ascription of a spiritual mind to the child. Both Mason (2008, p. 13) and Hart (2004a, p. 42) invoke Christ's teaching in Matthew's Gospel about the need to become like a little child (Matthew 18:2–5) as affirmation of the special spiritual capacity of the child; Hart, however, situates this account within a broader form of trans-religious discourse by connecting Christ's teaching to the doctrine of *beginner's mind* in Zen Buddhism and the concept of Laozi as old child in Daoism.

The prescription that children can appreciate the world of nature through the observation of animals and the use of a nature notebook to record their encounter with nature complements the work of recent exponents of spiritual ecology. Thus, Mason's principle of nature as a source of spiritual nourishment brings to mind the work of the journalist Richard Louv (2012), who introduced the concept of *"nature deficit disorder* ... as a way to describe the growing gap between children and nature" (p. 3). Both Mason and Louv recognize the uniqueness of nature and its irreplaceability as a learning environment. Similarly, Mason's view that nature is a canvas through which we can appreciate God can be seen as anticipating the ecospirituality of figures such as Father Thomas Berry. Berry's (1999) statement "Our educational institutions need to see their purpose not as training personnel for exploiting the Earth but as guiding students toward an intimate relationship with the Earth" (p. x) might be viewed as a contemporary ecological version of Mason's view that God is appreciated through nature.

Finally, Mason's views can be seen as part of a tendency through which spirituality operates in dynamic tension with the prevailing cultural forces of history and of the present. Mason's negative assessment of the rationalistic heritage of the Enlightenment can be considered to align with Hart's critique of the dominance of rational linear thinking within education and Western civilization at large; their views in fact come close to convergence through their concerns about the way in which Spencerian Social Darwinism has fostered an individualist competitive disposition within education and the broader society. In addition, Mason's (1886–1925/2008) view of the state of education in her time as "rather bleak at home and abroad" (p. 138), on account of its technical and utilitarian focus, reflects Hart's critique of an educational regime which encourages extrinsically motivated learning, as well as Hay and Nye's concerns about the sidelining of spirituality in education. Aligning all these different perspectives is a view of spirituality as a practice that serves as an antidote to instrumentalist, functional approaches to learning.

Conclusion

"We conclude that God is first known through Nature, and then again, more particularly, by doctrine; by Nature in His works, and by doctrine in His revealed Word" (Bartlett and McGlynn, 2014, p. 239). This statement, which has traditionally been attributed to the third-century Christian theologian Tertullian, reflects a longstanding reverence within Christian thought for nature as a source of human knowledge of the divine. In light of this tradition, it is unsurprising that Mason viewed nature-based spirituality to be of fundamental importance to the development and well-being of the child. Her engagement with this area situates her thinking at an early point within the historical trajectory of educational thinking and practice in this field. Such an approach is informed by a particular understanding of the child as one who has a privileged spiritual perspective and capacity. This view of the child can be considered to be the essence of Mason's theological anthropology—namely, one that downplays the principle of innate sinfulness and, instead, emphasizes the child's insight, innocence, and potential for growth and goodness. Such a view of the child does not exist in a vacuum but within a cultural context that informs how education is practiced and how civilization unfolds. Like a number of her successors, Mason presented the process of fostering the child's spirituality in contradistinction to powerful cultural forces that could be considered to mitigate against faith and spirituality. Mason's view of all knowledge and learning as emanating from the divine stands in contrast to widely held positivistic accounts of knowledge as based purely in observation; it is this very perspective on knowledge that aligns Mason's thought to that of certain contemporary educational theorists who critique what they perceive as the predominance of functionalist approaches to education.

In terms of considering how Mason's thought appertains to current educational practice, it might be useful to think about how her ideas can be applied to different age groups. When teaching younger children, Mason's view of God as a designer would seem particularly relevant. One way to foster this appreciation of God as a designer within the minds of children would be to present them with something that is a product of design (for example a toy) and something that is a product of the creative imagination (for example a painting of a scene from nature). Children could think and talk about the processes that were used to design the toy and produce the painting and, in doing so, develop an enhanced appreciation of the intelligence and skills integral to design and creativity. This activity could be followed by reflection on something from the natural world—for example, a plant. Here children could be encouraged to think about the kind of mind that would design something as beautiful and complex as a plant; this could be undertaken with reference to some of Mason's writings on the topic of God as designer. (The notion of divine design and God's close proximity to Creation is, for example, powerfully expressed in Mason's Home Education series, where she represents the mother as the interpreter of nature to the child and God as connected to nature through divine creative thought: "she will point to some lovely flower or gracious tree, not only as a beautiful work, but a beautiful thought of God, in which we may believe He finds continual pleasure" (Mason, 1886–1925/2008, p. 35). Having undertaken this activity in the classroom, children could be encouraged to apply what they have learned to activities outside of the classroom; for example, they could be encouraged to look at things in the natural world and think about how these things can be considered to point to a creative power beyond them.

Older children might be encouraged to reflect on their earlier childhood by exploring Mason's concept of the special spiritual status of small children. Mason's teaching on the subject could be undertaken with reference to poems such as Wordsworth's "Intimations of Immortality" and "My Heart Leaps Up," William Blake's *Songs of Innocence and Experience*, and Christ's teaching that we should become like small children to enter heaven. The key themes here could be: What is it about small children that lends them to be perceived in such a way? What does childhood spirituality mean and how does it differ from that of adults? Here it might be possible to explore qualities such as innocence, trust, dependence, and the way in which these reflect our need for connection. This in turn could provide a basis on which to explore broader accounts of spirituality—for example, that represented by de Souza, which sees spiritual experience in terms of deep connection. Here children could be encouraged to think of occasions when they have experienced a deep sense of connection or special moments of insight; this in turn could lead to an exploration of some of the practices of the great spiritual figures of history.

Finally, more mature children might reflect on the contrast between Mason's account of the spiritual and her critique of secular rationalism; this would enable children to be aware of different worldviews. There could be an exploration of different types of worldviews and the ways in which such views can clash with each other—as for example, positivistic atheism and theistic spirituality. Children could be introduced to the ideas of figures such as Hart, Hay, and Nye via Mason in order to explore the complex relationship between spirituality and rationalism. An exploration of this clash might lead, first, to a consideration of the concept of spiritual intelligence, expressed through a deep sense of connection to a dimension or practice that lends a sense of meaning and fulfilment and, second, to consideration of the way in which spiritual intelligence could complement other forms of intelligence such as analytical intelligence and emotional intelligence.

For such approaches to be successful, it would be useful for trainee teachers and teachers to be aware of the recent history of spiritually based education, beginning with the likes of Froebel and Mason, up to the present. While much work has been done on the importance of integrating approaches to spirituality into education, there appears to be relatively little that has been written on the historical development of the teaching of spirituality in the classroom, particularly with reference to the identity of the child. This omission is unfortunate because it prevents teachers from connecting present-day practice and theory to a tradition of practice. Scholarship in this area would enhance teachers' understanding of how spirituality can be applied to present-day educational practice and better enable teachers to impart techniques that foster deeper levels of spiritual awareness in the classroom and beyond.

References

Ayala, F. J. (2007). The Vatican and evolution [Review of the book *Negotiating Darwin: The Vatican confronts evolution 1877–1902*, by M. Artigas, T. F. Glick, & R. A. Martínez]. *History and Philosophy of the Life Sciences, 29*(2), 225–229.

Bartlett, K. R., McGlynn, M. (2014). *The Renaissance and Reformation in Northern Europe*. University of Toronto Press.

Berry, T. (1999). *The great work: Our way into the future*. Bell Tower.

Bertolino, F., & Filippa, M. (2021). The pedagogy of nature according to Maria Montessori. *Ricerche Di Pedagogia e Didattica, 16*(2), 133–147. https://doi.org/10.6092/issn.1970-2221/12192

Cook, D. (2011). Bodies of scholarship: Witnessing the library in late-Victorian fiction. *Victorian Literature and Culture, 39*(1), 107–125. https://doi.org/10.1017/S106015031000029X

Deck, M. (1910–1911). [Student Nature Notebook]. (CMC Box 32, File 519, Modes ALMC1958.400). The Armitt Museum and Library.

de Souza, M. (2016a). The spiritual dimension of education–Addressing issues of identity and belonging. *Discourse and Communication for Sustainable Education, 7*(1), 125–138. https://doi.org/10.1515/dcse-2016-0009

de Souza, M. (2016b). *Spirituality in education in a global, pluralised world*. Routledge.

de Souza, M. (2017). The complex reasons for missing spirituality. *Democracy and Education, 25*(1), 1–7. https://democracyeducationjournal.org/cgi/viewcontent.cgi?article=1295&context=home

de Souza, M. (2018). *A concept of human spirituality*. https://www.childrenspirituality.org/wp-content/uploads/2018/10/concept-of-spirituality.pdf

Hart, T. (2003). *The secret spiritual world of children*. Inner Ocean Publishing.

Hart, T. (2004a). The mystical child: Glimpsing the spiritual world of children. *ENCOUNTER: Education for Meaning and Social Justice, 17*(2), 38–49. https://www.westga.edu/share/documents/pubs/000471_94.pdf

Hart, T. (2004b). Opening the contemplative mind in the classroom. *Journal of Transformative Education, 2*(1), 28–46. https://doi.org/10.1177/1541344603259311

Hart, T. (2009). *From information to transformation: Education for the evolution of consciousness*. (Rev. ed.). Peter Lang.

Harvey, V. A. (1961). D. F. Strauss' *Life of Jesus* revisited. *Church History, 30*(2), 191–211. https://doi.org/10.2307/3161972

Hay, D., & Nye, R. (2006). *The spirit of the child*. Jessica Kingsley Publishers. (Original work published 1998)

Hedley, J. C. (1871). Evolution and faith. *The Dublin Review, 17*, 1–40.

Hodge, C. (1874). *What is Darwinism?* Scribner Armstrong.

Jones, R. H. (2012). *For the glory of God: The role of Christianity in the rise and development of modern science.* University Press of America.

Lightman, B. (2010). Darwin and the popularization of evolution. *Notes and records of the royal Society of London, 64*(1), 5–24. https://doi.org/10.1098/rsnr.2009.0007

Linstrum, E. (2010). Strauss's "Life of Jesus": Publication and the politics of the German public sphere. *Journal of the History of Ideas, 71*(4), 593–616. https://www.jstor.org/stable/40925951

Louv, R. (2012). *The nature principle: Reconnecting with life in a virtual age.* Algonquin Books.

Mason, C. M. (n.d.-a). *Ourselves, our Souls and Bodies – The Instructed Conscience – Nature - Science – Art – Sociology – Philosophy.* [Handwritten manuscript and proofs – before no. 1 to page 126]. (CMC Box 4, File 36, Modes 2017.466.9). The Armitt Museum and Library.

Mason, C. M. (n.d.-b). "Unto us a child is born" in *Childhood's estate and other poems.* [Handwritten poem]. (CMC Box 3, File 33, Modes 2017.457.1). The Armitt Museum and Library.

Mason, C. M. (1888/9). [Draft letter/article signed 'May Hendry' 1888/9]. (CMC Box 3, File 33, Modes No. 2017.460.1). The Armitt Museum and Library.

Mason, C. M. (1921). *Ourselves* (Vols. 1 and 2). Kegan Paul. (Original work published 1905)

Mason, C. M. (2008). *The original home schooling series.* Wilder Publications. (Original work published 1886–1925)

Mason, C. M. (2011). *Scale How meditations.* Lulu.com. (Original work published 1898)

Miller, J. P. (2010). Educating for wisdom. In E. J. Brantmeier, J. Lin, & J. P, Miller (Eds.), *Spirituality, religion, and peace education* (pp. 261–276). Information Age Publishing.

Mivart, G. J. (1871). *On the genesis of species*. Appleton and Company.

Schork, R. J. (1989). Victorian hagiography: A pattern of allusions in "Robert Elsmere" and "Helbeck of Bannisdale." *Studies in the Novel, 21*(3), 292–304.

Spencer, H. (1864). *The principles of biology* (Vol. 1). Williams and Norgate.

Ward, H. (1987). Robert Elsmere (R. Ashton, Ed.). Oxford University Press. (Original work published 1888)

Wilberforce, S. (1860). Review of *On the origin of species, by means of natural selection; or The preservation of favoured races in the struggle for life*. By Charles Darwin, M.A., F.R.S. *The Quarterly Review 108*, 225–264.

Wilson, R. A. (2010, September/October). The spiritual life of children. *Exchange Magazine*, 24–27. https://www.childcareexchange.com/library/5019524.pdf

Appendix A

Mason's 20 Principles

1. Children are born *persons*.
2. They are not born either good or bad, but with possibilities for good and for evil.
3. The principles of authority on the one hand, and of obedience on the other, are natural, necessary and fundamental; but—
4. These principles are limited by the respect due to the personality of children, which must not be encroached upon, whether by the direct use of fear or love, suggestion or influence, or by undue play upon any one natural desire.
5. Therefore, we are limited to three educational instruments—the atmosphere of environment, the discipline of habit, and the presentation of living ideas. The P.N.E.U. Motto is: "Education is an atmosphere, a discipline, and a life."
6. When we say that "*education is an atmosphere*," we do not mean that a child should be isolated in what may be called a 'child-environment' especially adapted and prepared, but that we should take into account the educational value of his natural home atmosphere, both as regards persons and things, and should let him live freely among his proper conditions. It stultifies a child to bring down his world to the 'child's' level.

7. By "education is a discipline," we mean the discipline of habits, formed definitely and thoughtfully, whether habits of mind or body. Physiologists tell us of the adaptation of brain structures to habitual lines of thought, *i.e.*, to our habits.

8. In saying that "*education is a life*," the need of intellectual and moral as well as of physical sustenance is implied. The mind feeds on ideas, and therefore children should have a generous curriculum.

9. We hold that the child's mind is no mere *sac* to hold ideas; but is rather, if the figure may be allowed, a spiritual *organism*, with an appetite for all knowledge. This is its proper diet, with which it is prepared to deal; and which it can digest and assimilate as the body does foodstuffs.

10. Such a doctrine as *e.g.* the Herbartian, that the mind is a receptacle, lays the stress of Education (the preparation of knowledge in enticing morsels duly ordered) upon the teacher. Children taught on this principle are in danger of receiving much teaching with little knowledge; and the teacher's axiom is "what a child learns matters less than how he learns it."

11. But we, believing that the normal child has powers of mind which fit him to deal with all knowledge proper to him, give him a full and generous curriculum; taking care only that all knowledge offered him is vital, that is, that facts are not presented without their informing ideas. Out of this conception comes our principle that,—

12. "*Education is the Science of Relations*"; that is, that a child has natural relations with a vast number of things and thoughts: so we train him upon physical exercises, nature lore, handicrafts, science and art, and upon *many living* books, for we

know that our business is not to teach him all about anything, but to help him to make valid as many as may be of—
"Those first-born affinities
That fit our new existence to existing things."

13. In devising a SYLLABUS for a normal child, of whatever social class, three points must be considered:—

(*a*) He requires *much* knowledge, for the mind needs sufficient food as much as does the body.

(*b*) The knowledge should be various, for sameness in mental diet docs not create appetite (*i.e.*, curiosity).

(*c*) Knowledge should be communicated in well-chosen language, because his attention responds naturally to what is conveyed in literary form.

14. As knowledge is not assimilated until it is reproduced, children should 'tell back' after a single reading or hearing: or should write on some part of what they have read.

15. A *single reading* is insisted on, because children have naturally great power of attention; but this force is dissipated by the re-reading of passages, and also, by questioning, summarising, and the like.

Acting upon these and some other points in the behaviour of mind, we find that *the educability of children is enormously greater than has hitherto been supposed*, and is but little dependent on such circumstances as heredity and environment.

Nor is the accuracy of this statement limited to clever children or to children of the educated classes: thousands of children in Elementary Schools respond freely to this method, which is based on the *behaviour of mind*.

16. There are two guides to moral and intellectual self- management to offer to children, which we may call 'the way of the will' and 'the way of the reason.'

17. *The way of the will*: Children should be taught, (*a*) to distinguish between 'I want' and 'I will.' (*b*) That the way to will effectively is to turn our thoughts from that which we desire but do not will. (*c*) That the best way to turn our thoughts is to think of or do some quite different thing, entertaining or interesting. (*d*) That after a little rest in this way, the will returns to its work with new vigour. (This adjunct of the will is familiar to us as *diversion*, whose office it is to ease us for a time from will effort, that we may 'will' again with added power. The use of *suggestion* as an aid to the will *is to be deprecated*, as tending to stultify and stereotype character. It would seem that spontaneity is a condition of development, and that human nature needs the discipline of failure as well as of success.)

18. *The way of reason*: We teach children, too, not to 'lean (too confidently) to their own understanding'; because the function of reason is to give logical demonstration (*a*) of mathematical truth, (*b*) of an initial idea, accepted by the will. In the former case, reason is, practically, an infallible guide, but in the latter, it is not always a safe one; for, whether that idea be right or wrong, reason will confirm it by irrefragable proofs.

19. Therefore, children should be taught, as they become mature enough to understand such teaching, that the chief responsibility which rests on them as *persons* is the acceptance or

rejection of ideas. To help them in this choice we give them principles of conduct, and a wide range of the knowledge fitted to them. These principles should save children from some of the loose thinking and heedless action which cause most of us to live at a lower level than we need.

20. We allow no separation to grow up between the intellectual and 'spiritual' life of children, but teach them that the Divine Spirit has constant access to their spirits, and is their continual Helper in all the interests, duties and joys of life. (Mason, 1925/2008d)

Handwritten poem "Unto us a Child is born," by Charlotte M. Mason Note. Photograph by the author.

Appendix B

Unto us a Child is born

All his rest is on her arm;
She, his only shield from harm;
She doth his sole meat supply;
All his joy is in her eye.

Helpless, that is not his care;
A burden, she is strong to bear;
Fragile, will not she forespend?
Ailing, soft her love shall tend.

Jesus, saviour, Son of man,
Who camest, infant of a span;
Was Mary thy one mother mild,
Or art Thou ever born a child?

My trembling heart doth in one burn;
There, perchance, shall I discern,
Tho' the stall be all defiled,
The tender form of Christ, the Child.

Is there One, a little One,
Who lieth sweetly as a Son,
All His meat, the Father's grace,
All His joy, the Father's face.

Rueing not His feeble state,
Fearing not the ills that wait,
Safe, nor asking why, nor how –
Jesus, then, not I, but Thou!

Other fearsome inmates there,
Evil dragons, giant care;
Hope, joyous, sees them led in thrall,
This "Little One" shall rule them all!

—*Charlotte M. Mason*

About the Author

Elliott Shaw has a BA in French from University College, London, a BA in Theology from St. Peter's College, Oxford, and a PhD from the Departments of Religious Studies and History at Lancaster University. He began his teaching career as Research Fellow in Theology at Lancaster University; on completion of the fellowship, he took up a teaching position in the Department of Religious Studies and Social Ethics at St. Martin's College (later the University of Cumbria), later becoming lead for the Religious Studies program. In 2016 he moved to the Institute of the Arts at the same university to take up the role of leading the development of the Critical and Contextual Studies scheme. In 2020 Dr. Shaw left the University of Cumbria and took up a position as Associate Professor in the School of Foreign Languages at Qingdao University, China, where he teaches courses on writing and cultural studies.

About the Charlotte Mason Institute

The Charlotte Mason Institute is a non-profit based in the USA that helps educators—through its curriculum, conferences, publications, ongoing research, training, and social media—to practice Charlotte Mason's relational education. Mason (1842-1923), a British educator and philosopher, designed, developed, and promoted a relational education in a living environment filled with books, experiences, nature, and ideas, where the child is viewed as a person and the educator as one who cooperates with God. The Institute engages current educational research and draws on Mason's design for education and her life work, which included authoring six volumes on education, establishing a parent's union, a teacher's college, an educator's journal, and a curriculum. In all its initiatives and collaborations, the Institute, founded almost twenty years ago, is committed to a vision of a relational education for all students and all educators in all settings.

About the Armitt Museum and Library

The Armitt is a museum, gallery and library in the UK which explores the stories and heritage of Ambleside, its people and the wider Lakeland world. Originally founded in 1912 by historian and naturalist Mary Louisa Armitt, it was set up as a subscription reference library and later expanded into collecting significant works from notable people as well as residents of Ambleside. Some of the collections include fungi paintings by Beatrix Potter, the Charlotte Mason archive, art by Kurt Schwitters, photography by Herbert Bell, the Abraham Brothers and Joseph Hardman, as well as archaeological material from the Ambleside Roman fort. In addition, there are thousands of books, articles and early publications relating to the history of the Lake District. The Armitt is a Trust and charity, open to visitors throughout the year for general interest, research, and events. Funds raised are used to ensure the museum can remain open for the benefit of all.

About the University of Cumbria

The University of Cumbria's Ambleside campus in the heart of England's Lake District is synonymous with Victorian educational pioneer Charlotte Mason. From 1984, Charlotte Mason's House of Education, was located at Scale How on the Ambleside campus. Over generations, the University continued to deliver higher education and teacher education with, depending on the era, alumni from Charlotte Mason College, Lancaster University, or St Martin's College before the University of Cumbria was formed in 2007. Today the University of Cumbria is a modern university transforming lives and livelihoods through its learning, applied research, and practice. The University's Learning, Education and Development (LED) research centre focuses on supporting practitioners to develop research-informed practice and publish research that has impact on policy and practice. The Ambleside Campus's Charlotte Mason Studies contributes to the University's three pillars of people, place, and partnerships by leading and participating in internationally collaborative research, writing, and convening that connects Charlotte Mason's legacy with education today. The program includes annual Scholar-In-Residence appointments, conferring of research fellowships on international scholars with expertise in Charlotte Mason, publications, and hosting conferences.

Dr. Frances E. F. Ward
Charlotte Mason on the Abundant Life: Attention and Education for Character

James C. Peterson, PhD
My Genes Made Me Do It! Moral Education, Charlotte Mason, and the New Genetics

Prof. Lois Mansfield
Field Notebooks and Natural History Journals: Cornerstones of Outdoor Learning

Jen Ager, MA, and Heather Prince, PhD
Charlotte Mason's Pedagogical Approach: Embedded Outdoor and Experiential Learning

Dr. Adrian Copping
Engaging with Story to Engender Living Ideas: A 21st-century Charlotte Mason critique of teaching and assessing reading in the UK (and beyond?)

Shannon R. Whiteside, PhD
Narration and Retelling: Charlotte Mason's Living Method of Learning

J. Carroll Smith, EdD, with John Thorley, PhD
Relational Educational Leadership: Critical Insights from the Correspondence of Charlotte Mason and Henrietta Franklin

Jack Beckman, PhD
From Continuance to Dissolution in a Post-Charlotte Mason World: Four Principals' Experiences at Charlotte Mason College (1923-1960)

Deani Van Pelt, PhD, and Jen Spencer, BS, MA, EdD
Students as Persons: Charlotte Mason on Personalism and Relational Liberal Education